News on Sh...

A World of Shoes

People all around the world wear shoes. Shoes protect feet and provide comfort.

Moccasins

Japanese geta

2

In some places, people take their shoes off before they go inside special buildings.

Boots from Lapland

3

Weather Wear

There are shoes to suit all kinds of weather. Some shoes are designed to be warm and waterproof. Others keep feet cool.

This child is wearing snowboots and snowshoes to get around on snowy ground.

Fancy Feet

Shoes aren't just made for walking. Sometimes people wear shoes that *look* special, even if they aren't very comfortable.

Some stage performers like to wear very high shoes, such as these platform shoes.

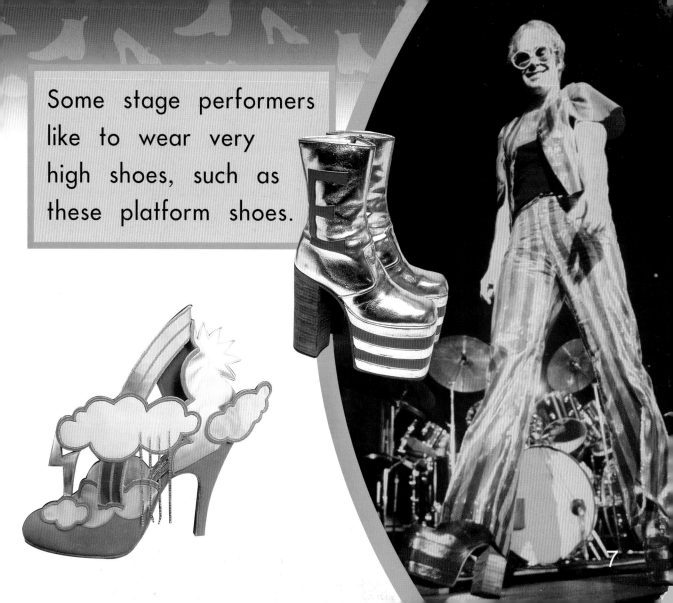

Footwear for Fun

Do you go running in slippers or swimming in boots? Choosing the right footwear can help you enjoy yourself.

Flippers are for
swimming. They
help "push" you
through the
water when you
kick your legs.

9

Buttons and Bows

In the past, people used buttons, bows, and buckles to fasten their shoes. These also decorated the shoes.

This boy's shoes have "shoe rose" decorations. These would have been made of lace and jewels.

11

Shoes for Sports

Whatever sport you like,
there are shoes for you!
They might have spikes
or other special soles.

Rock climbers wear special shoes with non-slip soles that grip the rock.

Let's Dance

For some kinds of dancing, you need special shoes. They might help you tap your toes and heels or dance on the tips of your toes.

Some dancers wear shoes with a hard, flat toe to help them dance on their toes.

15

Index